Tell Me About
SIKH GURUS

This book belongs to

....

....

....

Nita Mehta
Enriching Young Minds

Tell Me About
SIKH GURUS

ANURAG MEHTA

VANEETA VAID

Nita Mehta

Enriching Young Minds

Tell Me About
SIKH GURUS

Reprint 2009

ISBN 978-81-7676-068-3

Illustrations: *Nita Mehta*
Enriching Young Minds
Artist: Rajesh Prajapati

Layout and laser typesetting:

National Information
Technology Academy
3A/3, Asaf Ali Road
New Delhi-110002
N.I.T.A.
☎ 23252948

Contributing Writers:
Subhash Mehta
Tanya Mehta

Editorial & Proofreading:
Rajesh
Ramesh

Published by:

Nita Mehta
Enriching Young Minds

3A/3 Asaf Ali Road, New Delhi-110002
Tel: 91-11-23250091, 29214011, 23252948, 29218727
Fax: 91-11-29225218, 91-11-23250091
E-Mail   : nitamehta@nitamehta.com
             nitamehta@email.com
Website : http://www.nitamehta.com,
             http://www.snabindia.com

Printed at:
BATRA ART PRESS, NEW DELHI

Distributed by:
THE VARIETY BOOK DEPOT
A.V.G. Bhavan, M 3 Con Circus
New Delhi - 110 001
Tel: 23417175, 23412567; Fax: 23415335
Email: varietybookdepot@rediffmail.com

CONTENTS

INTRODUCTION

Our existence has always required someone to guide us. Living through life and carrying on with its various tasks for survival, sometimes blots from our mind the real paths to happiness. Then comes along someone, who not only is so special that his existence is hallowed, but apart from that, this someone fits into our lives with ease to lead us.

Guru Nanak was born to ordinary parents. However, he came at the time when the prevailing social conditions were going through a wretched phase. Guru Nanak was unperturbed. He knew things, that he wanted to share with the confused people. They listened. He made so much sense that people began to follow him. So wide and far did Guru Nanak's popularity spread, that it developed into a religion called Sikhism. Guru Nanak led the line of the ten Sikh Gurus, who succeeded him and further cemented a faith, which has become the fifth largest religion in the world.

GURU NANAK DEV

Kalu Mehta and Tripta Devi were blessed with a son on 15th April 1469 at Talwandi. They already had a daughter called Nanaki. "We must call Pundit Hardayalji to name our son," Kalu informed Tripta. Hardayal was the local priest.

When Hardayal saw the baby, he was quiet. After a few moments, he abruptly murmured, "Let me study the baby's horoscope*."

The parents were a little confused at the pundit's abruptness. Meanwhile, Hardayal sat down and stared at the baby's horoscope.

"This baby is no ordinary child," said Hardayal in an awed tone. "He will become a unique king amongst kings. His fame will spread far and wide."

Hardayal's words were prophetic. The child who was named Nanak, grew up to become Guru Nanak. Guru Nanak was the founder of the Sikh religion; the fifth largest religion in the world.

*Horoscope: a picture of what is going to happen to you, based on the position of the stars and planets at the time of your birth.

GROWING YEARS...

Nanak was no ordinary child. He had an alert and inquisitive mind. At a very young age, Nanak surprised his teachers and learned men with his questions and his maturity. Nanak did not just ask questions, *he gave answers too!*

Nanak enjoyed the company of sadhus and fakirs. He also meditated for hours at home.

Some incidents highlighted Nanak's remarkable existence. One such incident happened when Nanak was a teenager.

THE SNAKE UMBRELLA...

One day, a crowd collected at a field. People stood whispering in puzzled voices. What was it that caught their attention?

It was the sight of Nanak sleeping under the tree. He had brought his father's cattle to graze in the fields. Feeling sleepy, Nanak found a shady spot under a tree and slept.

At noon, the shade provided by the tree began to shrink. Soon, sun rays beat down mercilessly on the sleeping Nanak. Suddenly, a king cobra slithered out from no where. Nanak was completely unaware. *He was still asleep*, despite the scorching sun rays. Seeing the snake, the villagers in the vicinity, stopped in their tracks to stare. Meanwhile Rai Bular, the ruler of the city had trotted up on his horse and joined the villagers gaping at Nanak and the snake. Before Bular could shout and warn Nanak, the snake crept up close to Nanak and broadened its hood to the fullest.

It was obvious to all what the snake was doing. *The snake was shading Nanak from the sun!*

Nanak slept on, oblivious of this strange <u>sunshade</u>!

Dumbfounded, Rai Bular folded his hands and whispered, "This is no ordinary child!"

Rai Bular's words spread. Nanak was recognized as an exceptional child from there on.

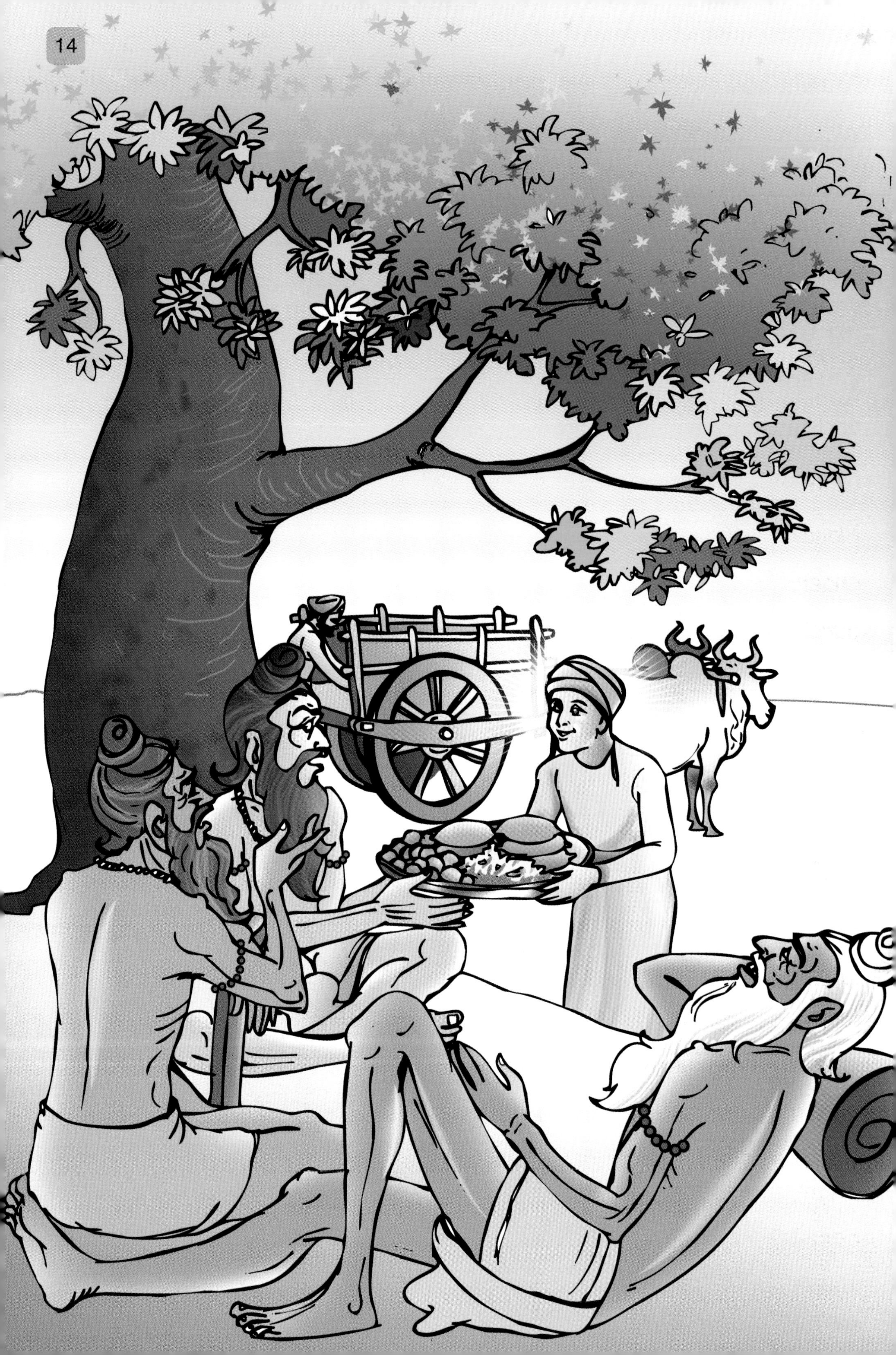

NO MIRACLES...

Soon people crowded Nanak's doorstep expecting miracles. But Nanak did not like this at all! Nanak believed in truth and the strength of logic. Unfortunately, rituals at religious ceremonies of those times had become a path to superstitions and money making ventures. Guru Nanak realized this. He urged the people, "Can't you see? All your food and wealth is going into meaningless rituals and sacrifices. With that money and food, help the poor instead."

NANAK IS THRASHED...

Nanak's quest to feed the poor once made him the target of his father's anger. This was when Kalu Mehta gave Nanak some money to make purchases from the city. Nanak left Talwandi early in the morning. As he made his way to the city, he came across a group of ascetics*.

"They look weak with hunger. This money is worth much more if I feed these ascetics," Nanak mused seeing the skinny *fakirs*. .

Without another thought, Nanak went to the nearest eating place and brought food with all the money he had. He quickly distributed this food to the hungry fakirs.

Happily, he returned home. Oh dear, Kalu Mehta, his father, was livid.

"You spent my money for nothing! You fed fakirs?" Kalu slapped Nanak thrice over in frustration.

Nanak was not deterred by this thrashing. He continued to set examples of good and sensible behaviour. Nevertheless, Nanak's parents were very concerned at his activities.

Ascetic: A person who abandons material comforts and leads a life of strict self discipline, especially as an act of religious devotion.

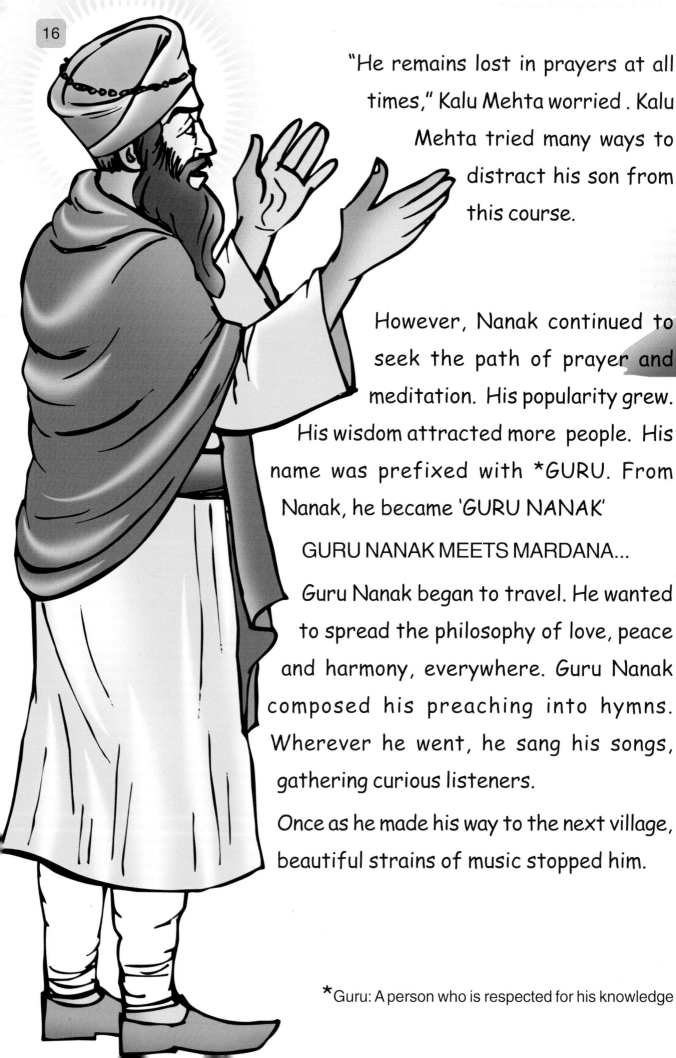

"He remains lost in prayers at all times," Kalu Mehta worried . Kalu Mehta tried many ways to distract his son from this course.

However, Nanak continued to seek the path of prayer and meditation. His popularity grew. His wisdom attracted more people. His name was prefixed with *GURU. From Nanak, he became 'GURU NANAK'

GURU NANAK MEETS MARDANA...

Guru Nanak began to travel. He wanted to spread the philosophy of love, peace and harmony, everywhere. Guru Nanak composed his preaching into hymns. Wherever he went, he sang his songs, gathering curious listeners.

Once as he made his way to the next village, beautiful strains of music stopped him.

*Guru: A person who is respected for his knowledge

Guru Nanak followed the strains.

He saw a lone man, deeply lost in strumming a *Rabab*
(musical instrument) under a tree. Guru Nanak was moved by the
sweet melodies being rendered. Conscious of Guru Nanak's
presence, the man stopped playing. "No, no! Please continue. I am
Nanak. I am impressed at your skill with the musical instrument."

"Thank you so much for the appreciation. I am Mardana," answered
the man.

For hours, Guru Nanak sat and listened to the tunes. Later, Guru Nanak and Mardana sat talking. Mardana was spell bound listening to Guru Nanak's ideas. A strong bond of friendship developed between the two.

"Mardana, will you set your tunes on the Rabab to my hymns?" Guru Nanak requested.

Mardana immediately agreed. From then on, Mardana accompanied Guru Nanak everywhere. He played the Rabab in the back ground as Guru Nanak sang his songs of God.

GURU NANAK, A HOUSE HOLDER...

Guru Nanak was married to Sulakhni at the age of sixteen. Sulakhni and Nanak had their first son in 1494. They named him Sri Chand. In 1497, Lakshmi Das, their second son was born.

Even though Guru Nanak proceeded to live the life of a house holder, he did not give up seeking ways towards gaining knowledge. At the age of twenty eight, in 1497, Guru Nanak made his first pilgrimage. Mardana went with him. They traveled around North India. Most times, people were suspicious and uneasy of Guru Nanak's strange clothes and preaching. Guru Nanak did not believe in the divisions of society. That is why the clothes he wore, were a combination of the prevailing Hindu and Muslim dress code.

"We are all human beings. Together we should unite to become a strong society," Guru Nanak would tell the people. His words began to have an impact. Guru Nanak's fame spread.

DUNICHAND LEARNS A LESSON...

"Ah! Welcome Guru Nanak ji, welcome to my abode. I can see the splendour and richness of my home startles you," said Dunichand as he welcomed Guru Nanak into his house.

Guru Nanak smiled and entered Dunichand's palatial mansion. They were at Lahore. Hearing about the esteemed Guru Nanak's presence in his town, Dunichand, a rich merchant, had invited him for lunch.

"I have so much of wealth…," Dunichand began to boast endlessly to the Guru.

"Dunichand, I want something from you," Guru Nanak interrupted the tirade. Dunichand eagerly said, "Anything, you say Guru ji. With my wealth, nothing is impossible."

"Get me a needle," said Guru Nanak.

"A needle? Guru ji? You ask for a mere needle? Alright."

Dunichand clapped his hands and one of the servants presented Guru Nanak with a needle.

"Dunichand, please keep this needle," said Guru Nanak dropping the needle into Dunichand's palm.

"What will I do with it?" Dunichand inquired in a confused tone.

"When you die, take it to heaven with you," Guru Nanak said simply.

"Huh? How can I carry a needle to heaven? No one carries anything to heaven. We leave all material things here on earth. You ask for the impossible."

Guru Nanak was smiling widely by now.

"Dunichand, why can't you take the needle? Take it along with the other luxurious possessions that you plan to carry to heaven after your death."

Dunichand immediately realized what the Guru was trying to teach him. He sheepishly apologized to the Guru for his boastful manners and gave away all his wealth to the poor.

SAJJAN LEARNS A LESSON TOO...

As Guru Nanak continued his travels, one evening, he and Mardana arrived at a rest house.

"What is your name?" Guru Nanak asked the owner of the inn, giving him a deep look.

"I am Sajjan," replied the inn keeper. Now Sajjan was not as straight as he appeared. In fact, he was quite the robber. He made money on the side by robbing innocent travelers staying at his Inn.

"Let the old man sleep, then I will rob him of his belongings," decided Sajjan.

But Sajjan was in for a surprise.

Guru Nanak made no attempt to go to bed. Sajjan impatiently waited. But the Guru remained fully awake. Finally, Guru Nanak called for Mardana and requested him to play the Rabab. Guru Nanak himself began to sing hymns along with the tunes.

Slowly, Sajjan's attention was arrested by the words of the hymns. They spoke of people who were robbers and cheaters. Hearing the words, Sajjan felt his body being stung, as if a thousand thorns had pricked it.

He writhed in pain. When he flung his head on one side, he saw visions of all the people he had robbed. When he flung his head on the other side, he saw the faces of all the people he had cheated.

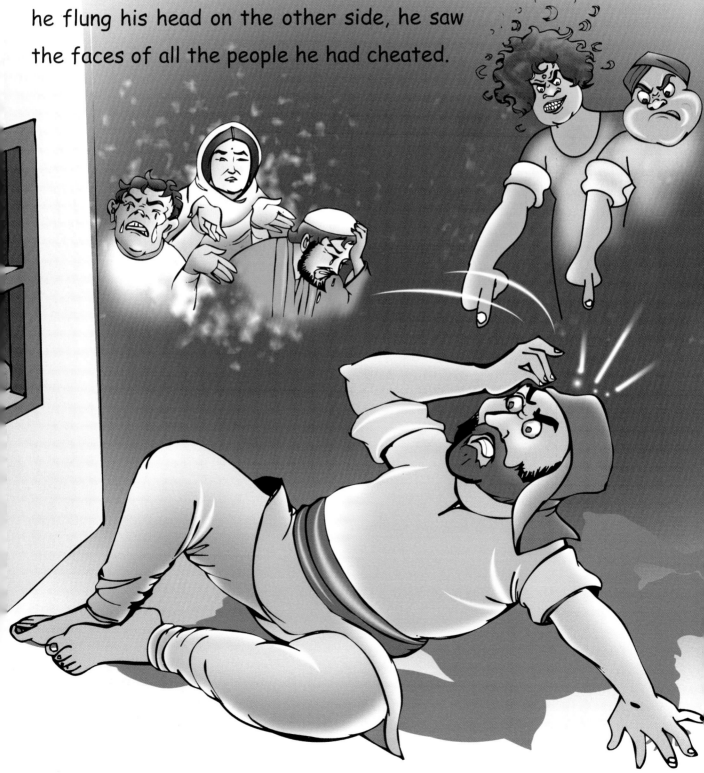

A mortified Sajjan begged forgiveness from Guru Nanak.

"You are someone divine! You have shown me my true self. Help me," cried Sajjan.

"Sajjan, only one thing can help you. Use your ill begotten wealth for the welfare of the needy."

Sajjan never forgot Guru Nanak and his visit. Sajjan became a devoted disciple of Guru Nanak after that.

GURU NANAK TRAVELS FAR AND WIDE...

History states that Guru Nanak made four great journeys, travelling to all parts of India. He spoke to Hindus, Jains, Buddhists, Parsees and Muslims.

He spoke at the temples and mosques and at various pilgrimage sites. Wherever he went, Guru Nanak spoke out against the futility of religious rituals, the caste system and the sacrifice of widows. He urged the people to depend on books to learn the true religion and to follow the other tenets that were to define his teachings. Guru Nanak traveled to Bhagdad, Iran, Turkey and Afghanistan, to learn the philosophy of other religions also.

But Guru Nanak's travels were not without amazing incidents. Once Guru Nanak had visited Mecca, the holy city of the Muslims. That is where the Holy Kaaba* is situated. Guru Nanak felt tired and decided to lie down under a tree.

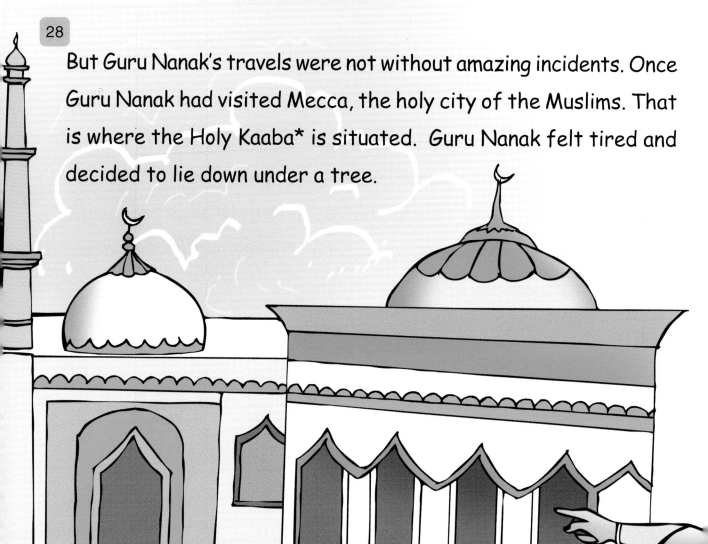

Two Muslim guards saw Guru Nanak lying down and were disturbed by his resting stance.

"You are facing your feet towards Mecca and the holy Kaaba. That is an insult. Move your feet to another direction," ordered the guards.

Guru Nanak settled further into his resting pose and smiled. He did not bother to move. Furiously, the guards flung his feet to another direction. But to their shock, the Kaaba seemed to have changed direction too!

*The Holy Kaaba is situated in the sacred city of Mecca and is a very precious symbol of Muslim faith.

Enraged, the guards flung his feet to another direction. But even in that direction, Guru Nanak's feet pointed towards the Kaaba. The guards were stumped. Sitting up, Guru Nanak mildly explained, "Dear people, wherever you fling my feet, you see the holy Kaaba, don't you? Did you understand the meaning of this?"

The guards shook their heads in confusion.

Guru Nanak smiled peacefully and said, "That means God is present in all directions - everywhere and in everyone."

Hearing these words, the guards fell to their knees, bowing in apology.

SULAKHINI ARGUES...

Guru Nanak's teachings brought him a lot of fame, yet he remained humble as before. A time came when he began to spend more time at Talwandi, the place of his birth.

"But our son should be your rightful heir*," Sulakhini firmly told Guru Nanak, her husband. Guru Nanak wisely shook his head and said, "Sometimes it is important to do the right thing, not an emotional thing."

This conversation happened after Guru Nanak had declared that he wanted to give up his position as a Guru. He did not name his own son Sri Chand, but a stranger called Bhai Lehna, as his successor. This shocked his sons and wife. Unable to remain silent, his wife protested. But the Guru's reply did not satisfy her at all. A silent rumble of dissent developed. These unsettled feelings carried on. Things were moving on to becoming a full fledged dissention. However, some incidents changed everything.

Heir : A person who succeeds or is in line to succeed to a hereditary rank, title, or office.

LEHNA PROVES HIMSELF...

One day, Guru Nanak suddenly threw his 'lota'* into an unclean pond. "Please retrieve my lota," Guru Nanak asked his sons.

Sri Chand, the older son, refused saying, "The pond is so dirty. Forget about the lota. I will get you another one."

Guru Nanak's other son, Lakshmi Das, also refused to retrieve the lota. Guru Nanak turned and asked Bhai Lehna, who was there too,

"Will you put your hands into the foul pond to retrieve my lota?"

Without a murmur of objection, Bhai Lehna jumped into the filthy pond. Sinking his hands deep into the muck, he salvaged the lota. He washed the lota clean and handed it to Guru Nanak.

*Lota: Metal urn

Later, relating this tale to his wife, Guru Nanak commented, "Our sons refused to enter a pool of grimy water to fetch the lota. So how will they rescue people from the dirty pool of their sins?"

Guru Nanak began to test his sons. Each time they failed, it was Lehna who passed with flying colours.

LEHNA PASSES A TOUGHER TEST...

On another day, Guru Nanak and his followers came across something that looked like a corpse wrapped up in a cloth. Guru Nanak stopped and asked his followers to uncover the corpse and eat its flesh. His shocked followers, including his sons, shied away in refusal; their faces expressing utmost disgust. However, Bhai Lehna came forward and said,

"Anything you say, Guru Dev."

He bowed to raise the shroud from the corpse.

Lo and behold!

There was no corpse there. Instead, there was very appetizing food! Lehna picked up the food and offered it first to Guru Nanak and then to the rest of the followers. After they had all eaten, he sat down to eat the left over.

Guru Nanak blessed Lehna and declared that he truly deserved to be his successor.

LEHNA BECOMES GURU ANGAD DEV...

Finally, Sulakhini also had to grudgingly agree that Guru Nanak's decision to appoint Bhai Lehna his successor was correct.

When Guru Nanak knew that his time to leave the earth had come, he called his family and disciples. Handing a coconut and a five paise coin to Bhai Lehna, Guru Nanak declared him to be his successor. He renamed Bhai Lehna, calling him Guru Angad Dev.

Guru Nanak had explained,

"There is no difference between you and me. You are 'Angad'- *ang* or a part of my body."

GURU NANAK SETTLES ON THE BANKS OF RAVI...

After the last of his great journeys, Guru Nanak settled in the town of Kartarpur (in Punjab) on the banks of the river Ravi where he taught for another fifteen years. Followers from all over came to settle in Kartarpur to listen, and sing, and be with him. During this time, although his followers still remained Hindu, Muslim, or of the religion to which they were born, they became known as the Guru's disciples, or Sikhs. Sikh means Learner.

Here is where the Guru introduced the common meal, which would be called 'Langar', requiring the rich and the poor, Hindu and Muslim, high caste and low caste, to sit together while eating.

However, when Guru Nanak passed away, a dispute amongst the Hindus and Muslims erupted. "We will take the body of Guru ji," claimed the Muslims.

"No, Guru ji was Hindu! We will take the body," the Hindus protested.

This scene took place over the Guru's shrouded body. In a frantic bid, someone pulled off the shroud.

GASP!

There was no body. It had disappeared. In place of the body, there were soft flower petals scattered on the bed instead! Even in his death, Guru Nanak had left a message saying, "I belong to everyone."

TEACHINGS OF GURU NANAK

- God is one. He belongs to all of us.

- Be honest and hard working and never be devious and idle.

- Share your earnings and help the weak.

- Never forget God's grace.

- The paths to happiness and contentment can be only found if you adopt a loving and giving attitude towards all.

- Believe in a sense of brotherhood and unity amongst all beings.

GURU ANGAD DEV

Guru Angad Dev was specially chosen by Guru Nanak as his successor when the latter passed away.

Guru Angad Dev was a resident of Ferozepur. He was born on 31st March 1504. His real name was Lehna. His father's name was Pherumal and mother was called Daya Kaur. Lehna was married to Khivi Devi in 1519.

Lehna and his family lived in a small village called Khadur, a village near Amritsar. Lehna had a full and happy life.

HYMNS LEAD LEHNA TO HIS GURU...

It was by chance that Lehna met Guru Nanak. This happened when once Lehna was bathing in a stream. His attention was arrested by some one singing.

"What wonderful words," Lehna thought. Later, Lehna curiously followed the voice. Further away, he found a man sitting under a tree, raptly singing hymns. Lehna waited for him to finish and then he asked, "Who composed these hymns?"

"My Guru, my most precious Guru Nanak," answered the man.

Saddling his horse, Lehna immediately went in search of Guru Nanak.

A STRANGER HELPS LEHNA FIND HIS WAY...

As he rode through a field, he saw an old man with a white beard.

"Can you please tell me where Guru Nanakji lives?"

The old man nodded to say, "Please wait here. Let me finish my work then I shall take you to him." Lehna was overjoyed.

Soon, the elderly man completed his work and led Lehna's horse to him. "Come," he beckoned to Lehna.

Lehna mounted the horse. The old man walked along leading the horse by its reigns.

Once they reached the main gate of the rest house, the old man left Lehna and entered a house.

After Lehna tied his horse, he too went inside the house.

"Where can I find Guru Nanakji?" he asked the disciples crowding the introductory passage of the house. Lehna was directed to a room on the side.

"Guru ji is inside. Please go in."

Imagine Lehna's shock when he saw the old man with the white beard (the guide who had ridden here with him), calmly waiting for him inside. In confusion, Lehna blurted, "Where is Guru Nanak Dev?"

Gently ,the old man said, "I am Guru Nanak, my son. Come in, you are most welcome."

Lehna was taken aback. He folded his hands and apologized profusely. "Forgive me Guru ji, if I have unintentionally hurt you in any way."

Guru Nanak smiled softly and replied, "You have come from far. You are an honoured guest here. It was my duty to serve you."

These words left a deep mark on Lehna. He decided to adopt Guru Nanak as his Guru.

LEHNA BECOMES THE GURU...

Lehna soon came to be called Bhai Lehna. He immersed himself in serving Guru Nanak Dev unconditionally. As years went by, Bhai Lehna became very dear to Guru Nanak Dev.

That is why on 14th July, 1539, Lehna was chosen as Guru Nanak's successor and was renamed as Guru Angad Dev.

Guru Angad Dev (1504-1552) is credited with the present form of the Gurmukhi script. What is Gurmukhi? It is and was the medium of writing the Punjabi language in which the hymns of the Gurus were expressed. Guru Nanak's hymns were composed in a language called Lande Mahajni. Guru Angad Dev modified the language by giving its alphabets a better shape and a new order.

The new script came to be called *Gurmukhi*, that is 'from the mouth of the Guru'. These scriptures were made available to the common people so they began to call it *Gurumukhi*. Like Guru Nanak, Guru Angad also believed that everyone in the community should be energized and active. There was no place for laziness and idleness.

HUMAYUN LEARNS A LESSON...

A very interesting incident occurred during this time. Northern India was being ruled by the Mughal King Humayun. But later, Humayun's kingdom was annexed by Sher Shah Suri, forcing him to flee. On his flight, Humayun was crossing a forest. As Humayun tiredly sought a place to sit, he noticed someone sitting under a tree. The stranger had his eyes closed. He was oblivious of Humayun's presence.

"Hey, listen stranger," Humayun called.

The stranger was none other than Guru Angad Dev. Deep in meditation, he did not respond to Humayun's shout. This angered Humayun so much that he rushed with his sword to attack Angad Dev.

Disturbed out of his meditation, Angad Dev opened his eyes and immediately recognized Humayun. By now, Humayun had trained his sword towards Angad Dev's neck.

"I am surprised that a king of your stature is drawing his sword on a fakir. It would have been better if you had lifted your sword against Sher Shah. Maybe you would not have been running like this," Guru Angad Dev calmly voiced in the face of this imminent danger.

Angad Dev's words hit the mark. A sheepish Humayun lowered his sword to apologize. Guru Angad Dev smiled, "Come, sit here, beside me. You have shown your greatness by apologizing for your mistake. I bless you that all your wishes will come true. Try once again and you will definitely regain your throne."

Guru Angad Dev's words proved prophetic. Humayun victoriously defeated Sher Shah Suri in a ferocious battle and regained his lost throne.

GURU ANGAD PASSES ON...

Guru Angad tirelessly worked against meaningless rituals and superstitions.

On 28th March, 1552, Guru Angad Dev left this world for his heavenly abode. Before his death, Guru Angad Dev chose his disciple, Amardas, to succeed him. The ceremony of the five paise and a coconut was repeated here too.

TEACHINGS OF GURU ANGAD DEV

- Guru Angad Dev believed in vegetarianism.

"Have compassion for the other beings sharing this planet with you," said he

- "Be good yourself," said Guru Angad Dev, "others will automatically follow you to the right paths too."

GURU AMARDAS

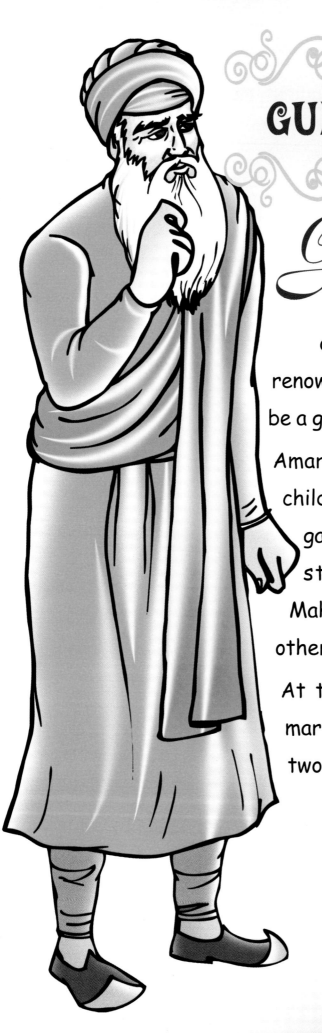

Guru Amardas was born to Tej Bhan and Sulakhini on 5th may 1479 at Basarke, a small village of Punjab. It was predicted by a renowned priest that Amar Das would be a great Saint.

Amardas was a keen and intelligent child. He grew up with a yearning to gain more knowledge about God. He studied the Ramayana, the Mahabharata, Puranic literature and other features of Hindu religion.

At the age of twenty four, he was married to Ram Kaur. The couple had two sons and two daughters.

AMARDAS SEEKS GURU ANGAD DEV...

One day, Amardas overheard his nephew's wife, Amro, singing hymns. The words of the hymns touched Amardas's heart. On hearing that the hymns were composed by Guru Nanak Dev, Amardas was very impressed. "Guru Angad Dev has taken over ever since Guru Nanak Dev passed away," Amro informed him.

Amardas immediately set off to meet Guru Angad. After meeting the Guru, he was overwhelmed. With extreme devotion, he began to serve Guru Angad Dev thereafter.

Amardas's honesty, sincerity and selfless service won Guru Angad Dev's heart. The Guru was convinced that Amardas was indeed the right choice to be his successor.

AMARDAS BECOMES THE SUCCESSOR...

One stormy night, Guru Angad called out to his sons and asked them to get some water from the river.

"We cannot go out on a night like this! It would be extremely dangerous," the sons said.

The Guru persisted saying that his throat was dry. The sons refused to oblige, but Amardas came forward and sought the Guru's permission to fetch water.

Amardas set out reciting holy hymns. On reaching the river, he quickly filled the pitcher with water.

On his way back, it was so dark that Amardas could not see anything.
He moved on, groping in the dark. He passed a weaver's house and
blindly fell over the weaver's loom.

The noise woke up the weaver's wife. Seeing Amardas, she said,

"How insensitive of Guru Angad to send poor, old Amardas to
fetch water on a night like this!"

Amardas angrily admonished her saying that she must be out of her mind to speak ill of the Guru. Holding the pitcher, Amardas went on his way.

When Guru Angad came to know of this incident, he embraced Amardas and declared him as his successor.

On 29th March, 1552, Guru Angad Dev gave Amar Das a five paise coin and a coconut. Then anointed him with tilak and declared him as the next guru. On Guru Angad's advise Guru Amardas left to stay at the village of Goindwal because Guru Angad had advised him.

REFORMS FOR WOMEN...

Amardas was over seventy years old when he became the Guru. He took many noteworthy steps. He denounced the practice of *Sati* * which was very prevalent in those times. He allowed widow remarriage and spoke against caste system. Guru Amardas vehemently opposed the *Purdah* * system too. Guru Amardas's philosophy bespoke equality between men and women. It was his belief that women needed more spiritual knowledge than men.

Guru Amardas allowed women to come to his gatherings without *purdah*. Soon, the *purdah* system was abolished.

* *Sati: the custom of a widow committing suicide by burning herself with her husband at the funeral*
* *Purdah: woman covering their head and face with a veil.*

These progressive viewpoints spread Guru Amardas's fame rapidly.

Guru Amardas continued the system of *Langar* or common meal kitchen. Nobody could meet the Guru unless he had taken his food in the *Langar*. The Langar system created a feeling of equality and brotherhood amongst the people.

AKBAR EATS THE LANGAR...

When the ruling Mughal Emperor, Akbar, visited Goindwal, he was curious to meet Guru Amardas. After having his meal in the Langar, Akbar met the Guru and asked him if he could do something for him.

To this, Guru Amardas replied, "I know you are the great emperor, Akbar. The only way you can serve me is by being a good ruler. A good ruler is the one who loves and cares for his subjects. A king must treat all his subjects equally with love and a sense of service. He shouldn't misuse the powers that he has and should be just to all."

Emperor Akbar promised Guru Amardas that he would follow his valuable advice. He presented gold coins and gems as an offering to Guru Amardas. But Guru Amardas refused to accept them. He said, "I cannot take this. Running the *Langar* is the sole purpose of my life. If I accept this wealth then my people will be hurt as the *Langar* is run by selfless service.

Please take this back. We only take small voluntary donations, not such large amounts."

JETHA IS CHOSEN...

One of Guru Amardas's disciples, was a young man named Jetha. The Guru was extremely fond of Jetha. It was not long before Jetha married the Guru's younger daughter, Bhani and became a part of his family. Soon, the Guru also realized that Jetha had all the qualities to become the next Guru and declared him as his successor.

Bhani proved to be a devoted daughter. One day, she noticed that one of the legs of the wooden platform that the Guru was sitting on, had a shaky peg. Bhani immediately balanced the stool by thrusting her toe. After a while, her toe began to bleed.

Seeing blood, Guru Amardas realized what had happened. Blessing Bhani and thanking her profusely, he asked her to wish for anything she wanted.

Bhani said, "Let the Guru be chosen from the family."

Guru Amardas did not expect her to make such a demand. But having given his word, he granted the wish.

Guru Amardas said, "It will be so, my dear. This seat will be inherited by one of our family members. From now on, this will be referred to as the seat of legacy."

On 1st September 1574, Guru Amardas left for his heavenly abode. Before this, he had declared Jetha, who would be called Guru Ramdas, to be his successor.

GURU RAMDAS

Guru Ram Das was born in Lahore on 24th September, 1534. His name was Jetha. Jetha was orphaned at a young age. He lived with his grand mother. His grandmother was a poor old woman with no means of earning.

One day, Jetha asked his grandmother to boil sated *Chhole* (chick-peas) for him. When she asked him the reason for this, Jetha confidently declared,

"I'll go around the village and sell chhole to earn money."

"No, my dear. You are too young for this sort of work," his grandmother gently retorted. But Jetha insisted she cook *Chhole* for him. With strength in his stride, young Jetha set out to create this new business.

Incidentally, Guru Amardas stayed nearby those days. When Guru Amardas met the young *Chhole wallah* (Jetha), he offered him a place outside his own shop. Guru Amardas was running a grocery shop then. Jetha readily agreed. Soon, a nice shady spot supported Jetha's *Chhole* stand.

Later, Jetha followed Amardas when he left for Kadur, to become Guru Angad Dev's disciple. Jetha remained with Amardas thereon. When Amardas was appointed the next Guru after Guru Angad Dev, Jetha's joy knew no bounds.

JETHA MARRIES BHANI...

Jetha was a very dedicated follower of Guru Amardas. Soon, he became the Guru's favourite disciple.

Around that time, Guru Amardas was looking for a suitable groom for his daughter Bhani. Guru Amardas chose Jetha to be his son in law. In 1555, Guru Amardas married Bhani to Jetha.

TIME TO CHOOSE HIS SUCCESSOR...

Consequently, Guru Amardas realized that it was time to choose his successor. Although he knew that Jetha had all the qualities and virtues of a Guru, he still put him through a test. The Guru called his two sons-in-law, Rama and Jetha and asked them to separately build platforms for him to sit on during prayer assemblies.

Rama and Jetha set to work and finished their platforms. The Guru told Rama, the elder son-in-law, that his platform was not built well. He should break it down and build a new one. Rama built it a second and a third time. But the Guru was not satisfied and continued to give the same orders, till in disgust, Rama refused to rebuild the platform.

The Guru treated Jetha in exactly the same manner. Jetha built and rebuilt the platform seven times. He never complained and each time, he rebuilt the platform with greater joy and enthusiasm. When the platform was made for the seventh time, the Guru blessed him. Jetha had passed the test.

On 13th August, 1574, in the attendance of a sizeable assembly, Guru Amardas bestowed the customary five paise coin with a coconut and anointed Jetha as his successor. He declared that from then on, Jetha would be called Guru Ramdas.

A LAKE FOR WATER...

The first task which engaged Guru Ramdas was to solve a major problem facing the villagers. Monsoons had not

arrived and there was no water. He decided to build a large new town with a deep, clear water lake at its centre. The lake would be kept full of water all the time.

Work rapidly progressed. Soon, a town as big as seven to eight villages developed. The lake too was built, right in the center of the town. The lake's pure water was attributed with healing powers.

Guru Ramdas also began to set up a temple on a high ground in the middle of the lake. This temple would be looked upon by the followers as the seat of spiritual and temporal authority of the Guru. This temple was called the HARIMANDIR and later the HARMINDAR SAHIB. The lake around the Harmindar Sahib was for the devotees to purify themselves before offering prayers in the temple. This lake was called the *Amrit-Sarovar* (lake of nectar). The city which developed around it was named *Amritsar*.

CASTE NO BAR...

Guru Ramdas constructed four doorways at the four corners of the lake. On each doorway, he had the words, 'Brahmin', 'Kshatriya', 'Vaishya' and 'Shudra' written over. This way he gave an open invitation to people of all castes and religions to come and bathe in the lake.

Although, Guru Ramdas started building the Harmindar Sahib, it was completed by Guru Arjan Dev.

Even today, Harmindar Sahib is an important pilgrimage spot for Sikh devotees. It is considered to be the major shrine of the Sikhs.

Guru Ramdas passed away on September the 2nd 1581.

Before his death, he had chosen his youngest son, Arjan Dev, to become the next Guru.

GURU ARJAN DEV

Guru Arjan Dev was the youngest son of Guru Ramdas and Bhani. In 1563, on the 15th of April, his birth was announced amidst many celebrations. Arjan Dev grew up, closely absorbing many lessons from his father. It was obvious to all that Arjan Dev developed a serene and saintly personality through these lessons. His way of working and behaving was quite different from his other brothers. That is why Guru Ramdas named him his successor.

"Arjan will be the rightful heir to this holy seat," Guru Ramdas proclaimed to everyone.

Sadly, Arjan Dev's elder brother Prithi Chand was very unhappy with the fact that he himself had not been offered the holy seat.

He was ready to do anything to dislodge his brother Arjan from inheriting the holy seat.

PRITHI CHAND'S EVIL SCHEME...

One day, Guru Ramdas was invited to attend a marriage in Lahore. Since the Guru was preoccupied with work, he asked his eldest son, Prithi Chand to attend the wedding. But Prithi Chand refused to go thinking that it was a ploy by his father to get him out of the way and install Arjan, as the next Guru. Guru Ramdas then asked his second son, Mahadev, who also refused. Finally, the Guru asked Arjan to attend the wedding.

"You shall attend the wedding. Return only when you receive my letter asking you to come back," Guru Ramdas told his youngest son. Arjan was supposed to be away for just a few days. However, Guru Ramdas's letter did not arrive so he could go back home. Months passed and there was no word from his father. Arjan though confused, did not want to disobey his father's instructions to wait. He began to send messages by way of letters to his father. There were no replies. Finally, Arjan decided, "I must return home. I hope everything is all right." On seeing Arjan, though Guru Ramdas was overjoyed, he demanded, "Did you not get my message for you to return?"

"No, Father," Arjan shook his head, adding, "I sent so many letters to you. But father, you did not reply even once?"

"Letters? Son, I received none of your letters. This is strange?" Guru Ramdas immediately ordered an inquiry to find out why he had not received the letters sent by Arjan. Investigations exposed Prithi Chand's plot. Prithi Chand would cleverly seize the letters before they reached Guru Ramdas. On questioning, Prithi Chand had to confess to his treachery. The Guru scolded him and said, "Prithi, you did all this merely to gain the holy seat of the Guru Sahib? This seat is not my personal property. It is Guru Nanak Dev's holy seat.

Only an eligible and an able person can sit on it. I have decided that Arjan would be my successor from today itself!"

A SEPARATE IDENTITY...

Guru Arjan Dev became the fifth Sikh Guru at the age of eighteen years. He would remain the guru for the next fifteen years.

He slowly gave Sikhism a separate identity from Hinduism and Islam.

Guru Arjan is also credited with the actual compilation of the Adi Granth, later to be called Guru Granth Sahib. He collected the hymns of the previous Gurus into one large volume.

Guru Arjan gave it a concrete shape by dividing the hymns according to their author and the type of composition and music. After the Gurus, the Adi Granth became very important as it represented the Gurus.

THE FIRST MARTYR...

The Mughal Emperor, Akbar, had cordial relations with the Guru. After his reign, Akbar's son Jahangir and grandson, Khusro disputed the Mughal succession. A battle ensued! Jahangir defeated Khusro in the battle. After his defeat, Khusro left for Amritsar to meet Guru Arjan Dev. The Guru told Khusro that though his house gave shelter to people of all castes and religions, he could not shelter him as he was involved in a royal battle.

Khusro understood and respectfully left. However, Khusro's forces had not even crossed Jhelum when he was taken prisoner by Jahangir's forces. Khusro was imprisoned and later killed.

Jahangir was given a misleading news saying Guru Arjan had tried to help Khusro. The Guru was accused and arrested for helping the rebellious prince. Arjan was tortured so badly that he died in the Mughal prison. Guru Arjan Dev became the first of a long list of Sikh martyrs.

GURU HARGOBIND

On hearing that his father Guru Arjan Dev had been killed, eleven years old Hargobind, was devastated. In his mind, he decided that the only way there could be a fair fight, in this unjust war, was to arm themselves. Thus, in the period of the sixth Guru, Guru Hargobind, the Sikhs began to change their entire outlook. From being a purely religious group, the Sikhs began transforming itself into an armed group capable of defending itself.

ANOTHER PLOT...

Growing up, Hargobind had a few unpleasant experiences with his uncle Prithi Chand. Prithi Chand never forgot his usurpation from the holy seat by Hargobind's father, Arjan Dev. He continuously plotted to kill Hargobind. One day, when Hargobind was a mere child, Prithi Chand tried to poison him by bribing the cook.

The milk served to Hargobind had poison in it. But fortunately, Hargobind refused to have the milk and it accidentally spilled. A cat drank the spilled milk and instantly died. Thus, Hargobind was saved and on investigation, Prithi Chand's evil intentions were revealed.

MIRI AND PIRI...

On 25th May, 1606, Guru Hargobind took the holy seat. During the ceremony he picked up two swords. He called them Miri and Piri. The Piri sword for spiritual needs and the Miri sword for wordily needs. The Guru also decided to have a kingdom, strong enough to withstand outside forces.

Guru Hargobind made some changes when he took charge of his mission as a Guru. He propounded the theory of the Soldier-Saint. He infused courage and strength into his disciples besides paying attention to their spiritual enlightenment.

THE TRAINING BEGINS...

He appointed special men who had the duty of collecting wealth needed for the Sikh congregation.

"I do not want money to build our wealth, but men, arms and horses to fortify the Sikh congregation," said Guru Hargobind.

Training of the young men in the art of weaponry and war began in camps. Guru Hargobind himself stood as a fine example of courage and skill and encouraged other young men to join the regiment.

His army had five thousand young men all ready to lay down their lives to protect their faith. Thus, Guru Hargobind gave a new direction to the Sikh way of life.

He also established the *Akal Takht* or the throne of God which served as a common meeting place for the Sikhs.

JAHANGIR IS WORRIED...

Jahangir, the reigning Mughal emperor, was worried when he came to know about the formation of the Sikh army. "Bring their Guru, Hargobind, to me. Forcibly, if necessary," Jahangir instructed his soldiers. The soldiers brought Guru Hargobind and imprisoned him. Later, Guru Hargobind was presented before Jahangir.

Emperor Jahangir asked Guru Hargobind many questions to which Guru Hargobind replied fearlessly. This impressed emperor Jahangir so much that he let the Guru return.

Presently, there is a large gurudwara in the Gwalior Fort, where Guru Hargobind had been imprisoned.

When Guru Hargobind returned to Amritsar, people lit *diyas* (ghee lamps) to welcome him. It was Diwali that day. Since then, the Sikhs also celebrate Diwali whole hearted.

When emperor Jahangir died in Lahore, his son Shahjahan took over the throne at Delhi. Shahjahan was a tolerant king. Guru Hargobind was a special guest at Emperor Shahjahan's coronation ceremony.

AN EAGLE CAUSES A WAR...

During this period, a strange event occurred. This event actually caused a war between the Mughals and the Sikhs. That too over an eagle! One day, Shahjahan's men were hunting in the jungle near Lahore. The officials had a hunting eagle with them. Suddenly, the eagle flew and entered Guru Hargobind's camp.

Guru Hargobind caught it and kept it for sometime. When the Mughal officials reached the camp to claim the bird, their arrogant behaviour angered Guru Hargobind. "You speak with such insolence. I shall not give you this bird," thundered Guru Hargobind in the face of such impolite behaviour.

"He refuses to give back the eagle," the Mughal soldiers complained to the emperor.

"Mukhlis Khan, my commander in chief will teach this Guru a lesson. Send him to attack the Sikh camp at once," Shah Jahan roared. Orders were carried out and soon the Sikh camp was under fire. But they were undaunted.

Even though a fierce conflict unfolded, Mukhlis Khan was killed by Guru Hargobind, resulting in the Mughals fleeing from the battleground.

There would be many such incidents where the Sikhs would lock horns with the Mughals. Every time the Sikhs would effectively stall any attack with valour and bravery.

Guru Hargobind remained on the holy seat for thirty eight years. When he realized his end had come, he declared his grandson, Hari Rai as his successor. Hari Rai was the son of Guruditta, who was Guru Hargobind's eldest son. On 3rd March, 1644, Guru Hargobind left this world.

GURU HAR RAI

The seventh Sikh Guru was Guru Har Rai. He was Guru Hargobind's grandson. He ascended the holy seat on 8th March, 1644, at the age of fourteen.

The first task faced by this young Guru was tackling the vicious enmity of the Mughals. Just like his grandfather, Guru Har Rai was expected to use the large army of the Sikhs to fight the Mughals. However, Guru Har Rai had a different approach. He was a peace loving man and did not believe in war unless it was absolutely necessary.

"We should defend the attacks with valour. However, we should never start an attack and garner ill will first," was the Guru's advice.

So, he refused to get into any confrontation with the Mughals. Guru Har Rai was gentle and hated any acts of brutality associated with war.

BE KIND TO NATURE...

Once, when Guru Har Rai was a child, he brushed against a flower, causing its stem to break. Young Har Rai was so affected by this incident that he began to wear his clothes tighter, making sure he never caused any damage to plants!

MEDICINES FROM HERBS...

Har Rai was known for his skill in medicine. He had a chance to spend his time in the Himalayas and therefore was familiar with various trees, shrubs and herbs. He studied these roots and learned abut their medicinal values. He became quite popular as the medicine man when he returned to his village. People came to him for cures. Guru Har Rai spent most of his time at a village near Sirmur.

HAR RAI CURES DARA SHIKOH...

With the passage of time, the Mughal emperor Shah Jahan also realized that the Sikh community was peace loving and posed no threat to his empire. He had also heard of the Guru's curative powers and admired him for it.

Once Shah Jahan's eldest son, Dara Shikoh, was seriously ill. Doctors from all over the country tried to cure the young prince but failed. Finally, Guru Har Rai was invited to cure the ailing prince. The prince recovered owing to the Guru's treatment. Shah Jahan was filled with gratitude for the Guru and extended his hand of friendship with the Sikhs. Thus, the relations between the Sikhs and the Mughals became peaceful for some time.

TURBULENT TIMES...

Time was taking very unusual turns in the history of that period. The Mughal king Shahjahan was arrested and jailed by his own son Aurangzeb. Aurangzeb's elder brother Dara Shikoh, who also had been named heir to Shah Jahan's throne, protested against the imprisonment. Aurangzeb set out to kill him. In order to save his life, Dar Shikoh fled. On his flight he came to Guru Har Rai's durbar.

"Help me, Guru ji! Give me your army to fight my brother Aurangzeb," Dara begged Guru Har Rai.

Guru Har Rai shook his head and said, "No! My army is not meant to fight wars. It is there only to protect our faith."

This statement was enough to send Dara on his way, away from the Sikh camp.

However, suspicious Mughal officers raided the camp any how.

The Sikhs successfully fought them off with an unbreakable united front.

RAM RAI IS OVERWHELMED...

You must remember, even though the present Guru did not believe in wars, that did not signify that the Sikh army was not in top condition or in alert readiness. Aurangzeb resented this. He vowed to somehow destabilize the Sikh unity. He got this opportunity when he decided to invite Guru Har Rai to Delhi. Guru Har Rai was uneasy at this invitation. Since he could not get over these unsettled feelings, he sent a polite letter of refusal through his son Ram Rai.

Ram Rai was overwhelmed by the reception he got from Aurangzeb. Cunning Aurangzeb, showering such hospitality, was of course a part of a larger plan, to rock the Sikh unity. But Ram Rai could not understand that. So, he happily accepted the grand welcome.

In fact, he was so taken in that when the shrewd emperor made insinuating remarks about Guru Nanak, Ram Rai, instead of retaliating, began to give feeble explanations.

On hearing about this incident Guru Har Rai expelled his son, stating firmly, "To please Aurangzeb you insulted our Guru and faith. Go away."

Thus, Ram Rai was forced to leave. He settled and established the city of Dehradun. Ram Rai unsuccessfully tried to raise an army to challenge his father, but no one wanted to join his army as they considered him a traitor.

In 1661, Guru Har Rai passed away, at the young age of thirty two. Before his death, he declared his five years old son, Harkrishan, to be his successor.

GURU HARKRISHAN

Guru Harkrishan ascended the holy seat at the young age of five years. He was the Eighth Sikh Guru. Although Harkrishan was just a child, he showed signs of enormous spiritual powers. Guru Harkrishan was selected heir at this young age because his elder brother Ram Rai had been expelled from the Sikh congregation.

Ram Rai was licking his wounds at Aurangzeb's court. He decided to take revenge for what he considered a wrong done to him.

With malice in his heart, he went to meet Aurangzeb.

"As a result of trying to please you, I was expelled from my own house, family and community. Now, I have also lost the right to claim the holy seat. You had once promised me that you would help me to get the holy seat after my father. But my brother Harkrishan has taken the seat. You must do something now," Ram Rai reproached the emperor.

"That's right," Aurangzeb said, "but what can be possibly done at this stage? You suggest some way to remove Harkrishan from the holy seat."

Ram Rai slyly suggested, "Please call Harkrishan to Delhi. Demand to know from him why he has gathered and maintained such a large army. Ask him if he is a king or a guru?"

CARRYING ON THE DEVIOUS PLOT...

Aurangzeb liked the suggestion and wrote a letter to Harkrishan asking him to present himself in the royal court. Aurangzeb summoned Raja Jai Singh and said, "Take this letter to Guru Harkrishan. If he comes willingly then its fine, otherwise you'll have to bring him here forcefully."

Raja Jai Singh was a friend of the Sikhs. He hated this task given to him by the Mughal emperor. However, he had no choice. Reluctantly, he handed the invitation to Guru Harkrishan at Kartarpur, where the Guru was staying.

That night, Guru Harkrishan summoned his advisers from the Sikh community to discuss the invitation.

After many discussions, Guru Harkrishan decided to go. The Guru said, "If I do not go to Delhi, then Aurangzeb will become Raja Jai Singh's arch enemy."

A Sikh regiment accompanied Guru Harkrishan to Delhi. People from all walks of life lined the roads to get a glimpse of this popular Guru through his journey.

"He has so many devotees," Raja Jai Singh could not help remarking to himself now and then.

THE MIRACLE...

However, Guru Harkrishan's popularity created waves of jealousy in the heart of Ramlal, a priest, who was present there too.

Unable to hide his jealousy, Ramlal sarcastically commented, "How can a child of five years, who is supposed to be playing around, be considered spiritually fit to ascend the holy seat?"

Guru Harkrishan smiled, then gently said, "O learned priest, when a person is in his mother's womb, at that time only, he is blessed by God. Age is not a barrier for gaining knowledge. If there is God's grace on a small boy, then he would have more knowledge than a grown-up man."

Ramlal arrogantly retorted, "Guru Sahib, if this is the case, tell me the meaning of the verses from the holy Gita."

"Even a deaf and dumb person can do that, if there is God's grace on him," Guru Harkrishan countered softly.

Guru Harkrishan instructed his disciples to find someone who was deaf and dumb. Ramlal at once called Chajju, a deaf and mute from the village.

Guru Harkrishan pointed his bejeweled scepter* on Chajju's head. This had an electric effect on Chajju. His body straightened and his face began to glow.

"Bhai Chajju, Pandit Ramlal wants to hear verses from the Gita with their meanings. Can you quote some verses for him?" Guru Harkrishan asked.

Chajju opened his mouth and the most amazing of things happened. A sweet voice lilted forth from his otherwise mute mouth. Chajju effortlessly began to sing verses from the Gita.

Everyone was shocked including Ramlal. He realized his mistake. Falling down to Guru Harkrishan's feet, he begged forgiveness, "I am your devotee for life, from now on."

After this incident, Raja Jai Singh also became Guru Harkrishan's ardent disciple.

*Scepter: an ornamental rod carried as a symbol of sovereignty

After a few days, Guru Harkrishan reached Delhi. Even though Aurangzeb had made grand arrangements to welcome Guru Harkrishan, Guru Harkrishan preferred to stay at Raja Jai Singh's palace.

Guru Harkrishan then sent a message to Aurangzeb that he had arrived in Delhi and the emperor could come to meet him anytime.

Aurangzeb being of a suspicious nature, sent his officials first to investigate what Guru Harkrishan was all about. The officials met the Guru and returned very impressed. Yet, Aurangzeb desisted from making a trip to the Guru himself. When the Mughal prince met Guru Harkrishan, he was over awed by the intelligence of the young Guru. He conveyed these feelings to his father, the emperor. On hearing such praise for Guru Harkrishan, Aurangzeb realized that he deserved to sit on the Holy seat.

"Your claims are invalid," the emperor told Ram Rai in a no-nonsense tone.

THE EPIDEMIC SPREADS...

Consequently, an epidemic of small pox broke out. There was chaos as the masses were affected by the disease.

The suffering people rushed to Guru Harkrishan. They prayed to him to protect them from the epidemic. Guru Harkrishan asked the people to read verses from the Guru Granth Sahib. But all this did not decrease the effects of the epidemic.

Guru Harkrishan could no longer see the miserable condition of the people. He prayed to God and said, "O God, if you really love me, then pass the people's suffering to me. Cure all of them and take away their suffering."

Guru Harkrishan then called everyone and announced,

"Fill a large tank with water. I beseech the people to drink water from this tank."

People immediately obeyed. Gradually, the pox affected patients began to recover.

THE GURU ABSORBS THE INFECTION...

Eventually, the people of Delhi were cured. But things would not end so happily. Guru Harkrishan was infected badly by the disease. It seemed that he had absorbed the illness of all his disciples. As his devotees recovered, the Guru himself became sick. His devotees were grieved, but had to watch helplessly as the Guru's condition worsened. On his deathbed, he whispered the name, "Baba Bakale," when asked who his successor would be.

Guru Harkrishan breathed his last on 30th March, 1664, at the age of eight. He had occupied the holy seat for just three years. His last rites were performed at Tilokhari in South Delhi. Now, it is called Gurudwara Bangla Sahib.

GURU TEGH BAHADUR

The ninth Sikh Guru, Guru Tegh Bahadur, was born on 1st April, 1621. He was the sixth Guru, Guru Hargobind's son. Tegh Bahadur lived at Kartarpur with his father. When Guru Hargobind formed the sikh army to combat the Mughal interventions, Tegh Bahadur, as a young man, participated actively in many battles that ensued. But all the killings and gross brutality that war entails, made Tegh Bahadur, sad and depressed.

The fallout of this situation was his total disinterest in worldly affairs. He shifted to Baba Bakale village in Amritsar district in 1644. Tegh Bahadur, spent twenty years there engrossed in meditation and religious discussions.

When Guru Harkrishan whispered his successor to be, "Baba Bakale," things fell into an argumentative state, since no name had been given. Twenty two hopeful men, including Ram Rai, rushed to Baba Bakale to stake claim to the holy seat. There was confusion in the congregation. "Who was the rightful heir to the throne?" was the puzzling question asked again and again.

A MIRACLE IN THE SEA...

Meanwhile, events which would have a great influence on this decision, were unfolding far away, in a distant land. A merchant by the name of Makkan Shah, travelling in his ship, found himself in the midst of a terrible storm on high seas. Frightened and panic driven, Makkan prayed to Guru Nanak, "Save me from this terrible storm and I will donate five hundred gold coins to the Sikh Panth*."

*Panth: Sikh Congregation

The words were still in his mind and suddenly the storm calmed down. His ship reached India safely. Makkan Shah gratefully made his way to Guru Harkrishan, to fulfill his promise of donating five hundred gold coins. On hearing that the Guru had passed away and everyone was at Baba Bakale; puzzling over who the next guru would be, Makkan Shah went there. Makkan Shah planned to offer five gold coins to all those gurus who were staking claim to the holy seat.

"Only the real Guru will know I had spoken of five hundred gold coins in my mind whilst praying," he said to himself.

Duly, Makkan Shah offered five gold coins to each of the twenty two hopefuls. They all accepted without a protest. He then made a visit to Tegh Bahadur.

When he offered Tegh Bahadur the five gold coins, Tegh Bahadur with a twinkle in his eyes asked, "You forgot your promise Makkan? This was not the amount you promised?"

Overjoyed, Makkan Shah ran out shouting, "We have found the true Guru! Come all and acknowledge him."

When everyone asked how he had come to this decision, Makkan told them the whole story. Every body was convinced that the actual guru had been found.

Guru Tegh Bahadur indeed had all the qualifications to be the next Sikh Guru. He had spent most of his life in religious pursuits. He had a saintly aura around him that immediately appealed to one and all. On 20th March, 1665 Guru Tegh Bahadur was proclaimed to be the ninth Sikh Guru.

NO ENTRY AT THE HARMINDAR SAHIB...

"I must go on a pilgrimage. I want to visit all my congregations," Guru Tegh Bahadur announced. He left for Amritsar almost immediately. We all know that the Harmindar Sahib, the main Sikh Gurudwara was situated at Amritsar. Alas just as soon as the priests heard that Guru Tegh Bahadur was coming , they closed all the doors of the Harmindar Sahib. But why would they do that? They feared that if Guru Tegh Bahadur would reach inside, he would claim all the wealth and power and they would be left with nothing.

When Guru Tegh Bahadur reached the Harmindar Sahib, the Sikh men accompanying him tried to enter forcefully.

"No! Do not force your presence on an uninviting host," Guru Tegh Bahadur calmly stopped his men. Without the slightest of ill feeling, Guru Tegh Bahadur made a comfortable place to sit near the Harmindar Sahib.

"Come, sit here," he said to his devotees. Guru Tegh Bahadur then began to preach. He spoke of Guru N a n a k and of the unity of the Sikhs.

He sang sweet melodies of Guru Nanak Dev's ideas. Many people gathered there to hear Guru Tegh Bahadur's discourse.

Guru Tegh Bahadur travelled far and wide. Finally, he settled at Anandpur Sahib.

"I will spread the philosophy of the Sikhs to the rest of the country from here," the Guru proclaimed. However, even as he kept a base at Anandpur Sahib, the Guru continued his travels.

AURANGZEB SPREADS TERROR...

Emperor Aurangzeb watched with growing unease, the rising popularity of the Sikhs. In his insecurity, he began to trouble the Sikh populace. He even started forcible conversions.

"Convert to Islam or die," he ordered the people.

Meanwhile, Aurangzeb turned his sights to the high caste brahmin pundits in Kashmir. He ordered the pundits to be forcibly converted.

"Let them be converted. It will set a fine example for others. If the pundits convert, the rest will do so automatically," Aurangzeb thought.

Horrified at this pressure, a large group of Kashmiri pundits met Guru Tegh Bahadur asking for his help.

THE PUNDITS ASK THE GURU FOR HELP...

Guru Tegh Bahadur advised the Kashmiri pundits, "Tell Aurangzeb's men that I am your Guru. If they have the courage, they must first try to convert my religion. Tell them that if they succeed in converting my religion, then you all would follow gladly."

When Aurangzeb heard about this declaration, he was furious.

"Arrest this pertinent Guru at once," he bellowed.

Guru Tegh Bahadur and his followers were arrested as soon as they reached Agra, in the due course of their pilgrimage. The Mughal officials brought them to Delhi, where they were jailed. There they were tortured again and again to accept Islam.

A BRAVE MARTYR...

However, Guru Tegh Bahadur refused to do so with determined persistence. The Mughal officials began to torture and kill Guru Tegh Bahadur's companions one by one. This did not deter the Guru. He still refused to convert.

Guru Tegh Bahadur was sentenced to death. But before that at Chandini Chowk, Aurangzeb prearranged the Guru to be squeezed into a cage and displayed on a raised platform . "I want the people to learn a lesson," said the emperor.

On 11th November, 1675, Guru Tegh Bahadur was brutally beheaded. To make matters worse, Aurangzeb ordered the Guru's body and head to be displayed separately at a public square in Delhi. Fortunately, two Sikh youths called Jaita and Dulo managed to extricate the Guru's head, carry it away from Delhi and fled before the Mughals could react.

Meanwhile, another Sikh youth, by the name of Lakhi Shah cleverly picked up the Guru's body and hid it under stacks of hay. Unnoticed by the Mughals, Lakhi Shah threw a burning match into the dry straws. The hay caught fire. To many this represented a funeral pyre for the martyred Guru. Hastily, Lakhi fled and the Mughals were left watching the flaming stacks of hay burn and consume the Guru's body. Guru Tegh Bahadur's head was given to his son Gobind Rai. In all solemnity, the brave Guru's last rites were performed.

GURU GOBIND SINGH

The tenth Guru, Guru Gobind, was born on 22nd December, 1666, in Patna, Bihar. He was called Bala Pritam as a child. How did he get the name Gobind then? The story goes that his maternal uncle, Kirpal Chand, would constantly refer to him as the reincarnation of Krishna and called him Gobind. Soon, every one began to refer to Bala Pritam as Gobind.

Guru Gobind was the son of the ninth Sikh Guru, Tegh Bahadur. Gobind's birth was heralded with a strange happening.

THE BIRTH OF A SAINT...

The legend says that Bhikhan Shah, a Muslim fakir, was meditating one day.

Suddenly, he saw a bright glow of light in the east direction. With his spiritual powers, he assessed that a great soul had taken birth. He said to his followers, "In the East direction at Patna, in a saint's house, our saviour has taken birth. I am going to see him."

The fakir traced the light which led him to Guru Tegh Bahadur's house. There he saw the baby, who later would become the tenth Guru, Guru Gobind Singh.

A FEARLESS LEADER...

When Gobind Rai was a child, he moved from Patna with his family. They moved to Anandpur, after Guru Tegh Bahadur sent a message asking them to come there.

Gobind grew to be recognized as a fearless leader. People were drawn to him because of this. His wisdom impressed everyone so much that Gobind descended to the holy seat at the age of nine. The date was 11th November, 1675.

His uncle Kirpal was his guide through these young years. When Guru Gobind matured, he made distinct changes to the understanding of the Sikh kinship. That was a period of turbulence for the growing Sikh community. Guru Gobind's father had been killed. Dissention was rumbling amongst the rank and file of the Sikhs. The atrocious circumstances under which his father died, traumatized Gobind Rai. He decisively made plans to fortify the Sikh *panth* against the Mughals.

A UNIFIED FRONT...

"I want us to be unified with a distinct personality which we can call our own," Guru Gobind announced to his congregation.

"Sikhism should change into an active movement to fight the dictatorship and injustice of emperor Aurangzeb."

His goal was to create a nation that would be pure and strong enough to free itself from the oppression of priests and rulers alike! As he ascended the seat, he realized the need for a strong Sikh army, that would be brave enough to face any torture or attack, valiantly.

He invited young men to join his army. Guru Gobind thought all the time about how he should shape the Sikhs into such a force that none could withstand it.

THE CREATION OF THE KHALSA...

On the day of Baisakhi, 13th April 1699, a significant incident took place. Guru Gobind organized a fair at Anandpur and asked the Sikhs to come armed on that day. He also arrived with a sword in his hand, raised his voice and demanded the head of a Sikh. The crowd of people was stunned. After some moments of silence, a man called Daya Singh offered himself for the sacrifice. The Guru took him into a tent.

A little while later, the Guru came out with a bloodstained sword. The Guru repeated his demand. The horrified crowd was silent till another man called Dharam Singh came forward and was taken into the tent. The same action was repeated a third, fourth and fifth time.

After five men were led inside the tent, the Guru threw off the cover to reveal that all of them were alive. Henceforth, the five men were called the 'Panj Pyaras', the five dear ones.

The next day the Guru administered the initiation of *Khalsa* to the *Panj Pyaras*. He prepared a drink called *amrit* for taking pledge. The Guru then announced a code of conduct and asked all who accepted the Khalsa to adopt the 'five Ks' - *Kesh* (uncut hair), *Kangha* (comb), *Kara* (a metal wristband), *Kirpan* (sword) and *Kachha* (shorts).

The *Panj Pyaras* soon became the leaders of the Khalsa sect. The sect grew fast with every family converting a male child to strengthen it further.

Guru Gobind also affixed common surnames for the Sikhs. The last names of the five were replaced by the suffix 'Singh' meaning Lion. This was to apply for all the Sikhs there on. The ladies names were suffixed by 'Kaur', meaning princess Lioness. By this move, all caste barriers were removed! Thus, Gobind Rai became SRI GURU GOBIND SINGH.

WOMEN HAVE RIGHTS TOO...

Guru Gobind Singh's influence was so much on the people that they were ready to sacrifice their lives. Guru Gobind Singh proved to be a progressive thinking saint. There is one such incident that highlights these traits.

One day, en-route to Anandpur, Deep Kaur, a member of the Sikh assembly visiting Anandpur Sahib was attacked by thieves who wanted to take away her jewelry. She fought off the robbers bravely; slapping, boxing and even knocking them down. Soon, her companions joined her and the robbers were dismissed. Sadly, after the robbers were sent packing, the group began to shun Deep Kaur declaring that she was no longer pure.

When Guru Gobind Singh heard about the incident and the aftermath, he was very angry. He called the entire group and said, "Shame on you. Who says that Bibi Deep Kaur has become impure? After fighting with the cruel robbers, she has become purer than the others. Every Sikh daughter must be like her."

FIGHT WITH THE MUGHALS CONTINUES...

Guru Gobind Singh moved from place to place, fighting the Mughals. He was a sharp and wise commander. The Mughals did their best to capture him, but failed every time. For some reasons, the hill kingdoms around Anandpur were aggrieved with Guru Gobind Singh. They decided to attack Anandpur collectively. The combined forces surrounded the Anandpur Sahib, but they had underestimated the strength of the fortress. Its main door was closed from inside

and it became impossible for them to open it.

"Only a drunk elephant can break through this strong door," they said. So, an elephant was brought in and made to drink liquor. Maddened by alcohol, the elephant battered the massive doors of the fortress with his head.

Guru Gobind Singh sent one of his commanders, Bhai Bachitra Singh, to deal with the situation.

Riding like a wind against a ruthless storm, Bhai Bachitra Singh swept out of the fortress. He raced up to the elephant and in one strong stroke speared it on its forehead. Wild with pain, the elephant swung around and charged at the enemies behind him! In this confusion, Bhai Bachitra escaped. Leaving the enemies running for their lives from the furious elephant.

The elephant attacked the soldiers of the combined forces. Many soldiers came under its feet and those who survived, ran away, back to the safety of the hills.

The Mughal emperor was upset on hearing about this defeat. He began to find ways and means to capture Guru Gobind Singh.

CONVERT OR DIE...

Unfortunately, in the battles that followed, Guru Gobind lost his sons and mother too.

Nawab Wazir Khan (a Mughal ally) forced the Guru's sons to convert. "Convert or die," he snarled at the sons who refused to bow their heads.

"We prefer death than listen to what you have to say," the young boys declared. "Plaster them into brick walls," Wazir Khan commanded. Sadly, this sentence was carried out immediately. This news shocked the boys' grandmother (Guru Gobind Singh's mother). A massive stroke claimed her heart and she passed away.

Guru Gobind, in-spite of these sad events, did not shy away from his tasks. He relentlessly continued to fight the Mughal forces. Things went from bad to worse and Guru

Gobind Singh moved to a safer place. There was never a moment of peace between the Sikhs and the Mughals thereon.

After Aurangzeb's death, Bahadur Shah ascended the throne of Delhi. He realized the gravity of the situation and decided to calm things down. With this purpose in mind, he invited Guru Gobind Singh to Agra.

Wazir Khan, who was guilty of murdering Guru Gobind's sons, nervously thought,

"Suppose the Guru complains to the emperor of my crime? I will surely be hanged," thought Wazir Khan.

THE MURDEROUS PLOT...

Thus frightened, he decided to hatch a plan and murder Guru Gobind Singh. He appointed a *pathan* named Gulkhan to kill Guru Gobind Singh.

One afternoon, Gulkhan attacked Guru Gobind Singh. Guru Gobind thwarted the attack and killed Gulkhan. But he was injured badly. His condition grew serious and his recovery was uncertain. Guru Gobind Singh himself began to believe his end was near.

He called his congregation and proclaimed,

"There will be no Guru after me. You all must respect and consider the Granth Sahib* as your guru."

A ceremony of anointment was initiated. Guru Gobind placed five batashas and a coconut before the Granth Sahib and bowed his head before it.

He said, "From today, Granth Sahib will be called 'Guru Granth Sahib'. Whoever wishes to attain the God, can read the holy book and achieve success."

On 7th October, 1708, Guru Gobind Singh breathed his last. With him, ended the era of the Sikh Gurus.

From then on, the Guru Granth Sahib is considered the eleventh and the final Sikh Guru.

*Guru Granth Sahib: The Holy book of the Sikhs